IN QUIET LIGHT

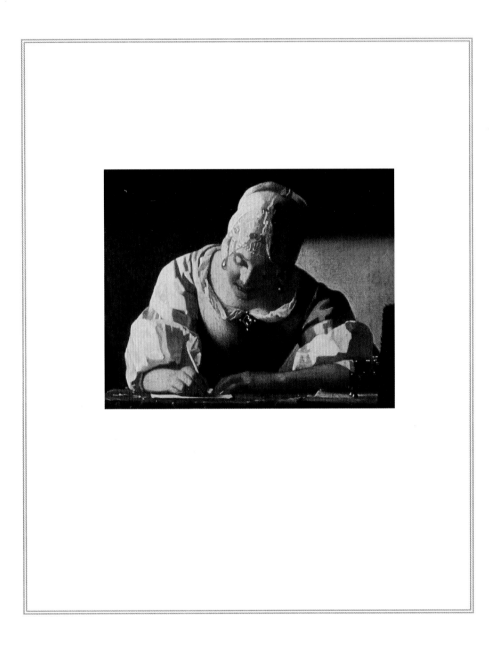

In Quiet Light

Poems on Vermeer's Women

MARILYN CHANDLER MCENTYRE

WILLIAM B. EERDMANS PUBLISHING COMPANY

GRAND RAPIDS, MICHIGAN / CAMBRIDGE, U.K.

In Quiet Light

Poems on Vermeer's Women

Text copyright ©2000 by Marilyn Chandler McEntyre
All rights reserved
Published 2000 by Wm. B. Eerdmans Publishing Company
255 Jefferson Ave. S.E., Grand Rapids, Michigan 49503 /
P.O. Box 163, Cambridge CB3 9PU U.K.
Printed in the U.S.A.
04 03 02 01 00   7 6 5 4 3 2 1

Library of Congress Cataloging-in-Publication Data
McEntyre, Marilyn Chandler, 1949–
    In quiet light: poems on Vermeer's women / Marilyn Chandler McEntyre.
        p. cm.
    ISBN 0-8028-3879-0 (hardcover: alk. paper)
    1. Vermeer, Johannes, 1632–1675—Poetry. 2. Delft (Netherlands)—Poetry. 3. Artists'
models—Poetry. 4. Women in art—Poetry. 5. Painting—Poetry. 6. Women—Poetry.
I. Title.

PS3563.C3616 I5 2000
811'.6—dc21

                                                    00-063611

Book designed by Willem Mineur

www.eerdmans.com

Dedication

To John
and to our children,
remembering gratefully how we are all
held in the light

Acknowledgments

I owe many thanks to people
who gave these poems
generous and intelligent readings and
offered astute suggestions along the way:
Josephine Carson, Diana O Hehir,
Patricia Leddy, Robert Chianese, Mediha Saliba,
Paul Willis, Deborah and George Hunsinger,
my daughters—Mary Rotelli, Elizabeth Taylor,
and Margaret Teichert—and my husband, John,
without whom none of the poems
would have been written.

In Quiet Light

Table of Contents

Introduction

THE FIRST TIME I saw a Vermeer painting "in person," I was visiting the Frick collection in New York City. As I stepped into a large gallery lined with paintings, one caught and held my eye. It was strangely, strikingly luminous, almost as though it had its own light source more concentrated and alive than the muted indirect lighting on the gallery walls. The painting, Vermeer's *Mistress and Maid*, seemed poised between stillness and movement, as were the women it depicted. The mistress, in a yellow, ermine-lined jacket, brilliant against the darkness behind her, is pausing for a moment, hand raised tentatively to her chin, considering. The maid, half-concealed in the darkness, leans toward her, holding out a folded paper, no doubt a message. We'll never know what the message contains, what the maid knows, what the mistress feels. The painting called me into a moment so particular and fleeting, and so charged with its sense of heightened but undisclosed emotion, that I crossed the polished floor with an odd feeling of urgency to stand in front of it, quite spellbound, no doubt obstructing other tourists.

I was young; I had to my credit one college course in art history, a few museum tours, and a passionate interest in literature that occasionally led me into the world of visual art—not much more. This encounter with a painting was one of my earliest and most memorable experiences of what Edmund Wilson called the "shock of recognition," which I have come to regard as a hallmark of an authentic encounter with what is true.

The term "truth" in art bears much discussion, little of which I'll venture into here, except to say that the term "the ring of truth" comes to mind each time I gaze at Vermeer's women and sense again how they communicate something deep and not wholly nameable about interior life, and about what it is to see with a clear, compassionate gaze, as the painter did. It is the same "ring" that sounds when I look at Van Gogh's shimmering cypress trees or Rembrandt's weathered faces emerging from a darkness that suggests long nights and North Sea winters which they have survived, burnished and glowing with interior fire.

Since that day in the Frick, I have spent many rewarding hours with the Dutch masters, whose work offers to let me in on a secret, to disclose something intimate and almost shocking about what intensities surge behind the surfaces of ordinary things. Vermeer, in particular, invites us into an environment rich with unspoken feeling. There is in some of his portraits of women a quality of unconscious self-disclosure that makes them poignant; they are hesitant, pensive, attentive, cautious, reticent, apprehensive, or deep in concentration. The viewers' vantage point enforces a kind of dramatic irony: we know something about them they do not—perhaps could not—know themselves. What we know about them is mediated by the intelligent, generous eye of the artist, whose work it was to enable us to see as he saw. These women are appreciated. They are the objects of honorable and honoring attention that endows them, their work, and the circumstances of their lives with particular dignity.

The Milkmaid and *The Lacemaker* were two of the first that caught my attention a few years ago when I began to give myself time to sit and gaze at reproductions, first those in art books, and later the largest prints we could find to hang on our walls. Perhaps because these figures fit no current category of feminine beauty or gracefulness—they are not lithe and slim, their faces are plain, and they have no "personality" beyond the quality of deep attention to their work that ennobles them—they are particularly touching. They evoke more tenderness than admiration—unlike the *Girl with a Pearl Earring*, whose beauty would challenge any standard.

The lovely, turbaned girl with the famous earring is, in fact, compellingly beautiful. I find her more seductive, baffling, ambiguous, and surprising than the *Mona Lisa*. I suppose most adult women carry in them some felt memory of what it was like to hover on the delicate turning point between girlhood and womanhood. And I suppose that for most of us that developmental moment was rich with ambivalence and ambiguity—self-protection and daring, deference and self-assurance held in tension. Vermeer's girl with her rich pearl (which, I was delighted to discover, reflects in miniature the panes of the window across the room) awakens that memory and allows me to renew and reclaim my original surprised awareness of self-possession. The young woman's expression and posture demand to be read, but don't yield easily to a single reading any more than young girls generally do. The painter seems to demand of the viewer a patience and restraint from judgment that one might do well to practice on any young women going through the vulnerabilities of growing up and leaving girlhood for the more complex pleasures of adulthood.

Reflecting on each of the paintings in turn, I felt I was learning something valuable and affirming about womanhood—my own, my daughters', that of the women I have known as students in college classrooms, hovering on the cusp of adulthood, restless and reticent, wanting to be seen, wanting to hide, loving their work, loving their own lovely selves, dressed and decorated or disguised in jeans and jackets. I recognized the innocent vanity of the *Young Woman with a Pearl Necklace*, remembering small girls who asked me "Mommy, aren't I pretty?" not to be reassured, but simply to share their keen pleasure in their own images in the mirror. Remembering the heaviness of late pregnancy, I took particular measure of the intense preoccupation of the *Woman in Blue*: at a time when any woman would gratefully accept the nearest chair, she doesn't bother to sit down, but bends all her energies to the cryptic paper in her hand.

Taken together, these women articulate a rich respect for and understanding of womanliness. In them I recognize the consent of this Protestant painter turned Catholic to the way the Roman church more explicitly honors the image of God in womanly form. They seem a radiant testimony to the painter's conviction that we are loved and held in the light. My affection for them has brought me into an enriching encounter with the mind of Vermeer.

The relationship I claim and enjoy with Vermeer is not a privileged relationship; it is available to anyone willing to stop and look. Though even the most expert reproductions can't quite replicate the impact of the originals, the dispersion of art by means of reproductive technologies has opened to a wide public a feast that used to be much more closely reserved for an affluent elite.

Art doesn't belong to collectors or museum docents or art historians, any more than stories belong to publishers or to those who teach literature in classrooms. Paintings and sculptures, stories, poems, and songs, although they are bought and sold, critiqued and discussed in elite settings by learned people, are valuable primarily because, if they are good and lasting, they represent the dream material of the culture and, like our personal dreams, have gifts for us if we are willing to receive them. If it does its work, creative art engages us in creative response. As Emerson pointed out, "There is creative reading as well as creative writing." If we allow ourselves to be addressed and awakened—moved or even puzzled—by a work of art, we are repeatedly, surprisingly brought to terms with something in ourselves.

Perhaps "being moved" is too passive a way of putting it. Good art doesn't take us by force; it requires something of us. In a certain sense, art always invites our consent. To pause before a painting is already a form of consent: we must consent to adopt a point of view that is not our own, a moment that is not now, a world that is the province of someone else's imagination. The invitation is something like this: if you will dwell here for a little while, I'll show you something you couldn't have seen otherwise. When you've seen it, you will be changed a little. Your feelings, tastes, judgments, and assumptions will be a little more complex, perhaps more difficult to name, richer than they were before.

"Dwelling," for most of us, is a discipline that has to be learned and practiced. It has become increasingly hard, in a culture dominated by movement and speed, where we get our visual habits from moving pictures or the rapid riffling of magazine pages, to pause and ponder the subtleties of a line, a ray of light, a nuance of color or tone. We must learn arduously what may have come more naturally in quieter times and places: to dwell on, dwell in, or dwell with an object of contemplation.

Good art will not allow us to take it in and dispense with it quickly or lightly. It mocks our superficialities and rewards our sincere questions with surprises. It instructs us, not only about the object represented but about the mind of the painter and about ourselves—this last if we bother to reckon with our own felt responses, pausing to consider how and why we are moved, troubled, or exhilarated. Art like Vermeer's that focuses on the human subject bears complex witness to the mystery of human presence, to something we might variously name as "spirit," "mood," "vitality," "energy," or even "love." If, in a special sense, such paintings tell the truth, the truth they tell is historical (in all the rich facticity that leaves a record of the Dutch Golden Age), psychological (insofar as one may regard these highly individuated women as "characters" with stories that led to the moment in which we see them), and theological (if we think of those moments as moments of grace). To "consent" to their terms is to engage in contemplation. It may even turn us toward prayer—or poetry.

The poems in this book are my own experiments in contemplation. It is a pleasure to share them, as it was a pleasure to spend the hours with line and color and language that took me again and again to quiet places of the spirit and led me to discover the contours of my own interior spaces. It is my hope that both paintings and poems will serve as open invitations into moments of repose and reflection, perhaps on some undisturbed afternoon in a quiet place where the light falls.

Marilyn Chandler McEntyre

The craftsman who made the rose window at Chartres
rose one morning in the dead of winter,
shivered into what layers of wool he owned,
and went to his bench to boil molten lead.
This was not the day to cut the glass or dye it,
lift it to the sun to see the colors dance
along the walls, or catch one's breath
at peacock shades of blue: only, today,
to lay hot lead in careful lines, circles,
wiping and trimming, making
a perfect space for light.

When Wren designed St. Paul's, he had to turn away
each day from the vision in his mind's wide eye
to scraps of paper where columns of figures measured
tension and stress, heft and curve, angle and bearing point.
Whole days he spent considering the density
of granite, the weathering of hardwoods,
the thickness of perfect mortar, all
to the greater glory of God.

And Vermeer with his houseful of children
didn't paint some days, didn't even mix
powders or stretch canvasses, or clean palettes,
but hauled in firewood, cleaned out
a flue, repaired a broken cradle, remembering,
as he bent to his task, how light shone gold
on a woman's flesh, and gathered
in drops on her pearls.

Women work, children play, and in the antique quiet
of the little street every sound echoes.
No white noise here, only white
light and human voices.

Children giggle over their game.
Water gurgles in the courtyard fountain.
The low hum of the seamstress lingers
in the mind of a passerby.

She looks to her occupation; she doesn't notice
the vast sky casting its shadowy portents
over the rooftops or the sudden breeze
that shoots a memory of winter up
the very spines of the sunbeams.

Behind the right angles, beyond
the steep roofs that shelter quiet lives
in filtered light, polished pewter and thick rugs,
linens folded and washed and wooden tables,
women who sew and men who write
or draw or paint or drink their evening pint,

Above the one who bends to wring her cleaning rags
in the fountain, the wide sky circles,
curved and turning.

Nothing is straight up there, or single.

The same light that falls through
windowframes warms the bent back,
dances deftly as a painter's brush
on the rusty surface of reassuring brick
and makes a halo of the matron's cap.

Little Street

Her hands know what to do:
they dance, winding the threads
around their tiny maypoles, tying
each knot with surprising speed under
the deep calm of that broad, honest face,
suspended like a benevolent moon
over this delicate task.

She is not delicate. Body and bosom
are full-fleshed; her heavy ringlets will uncurl
by sundown. Wool and wood, metal hooks
and folds of yellow fabric are rich
with gravity and mass—things
solidly of this world.

The
Lacemaker

Yet in this light that pours
from some high window,
passing beneficence of a northern sun,
those solid things seem fragile:
the light will shift; she will lift her head
and stretch and sigh, the quiet
around her rippled like a pond's surface,
and this graced moment gone.

Gathered on what we see,
filtered through lace, gleaming
on hair and polished wood, what we see
is always the light.

The Milkmaid

There is no flattery here: this thick-
muscled, broad-bottomed girl has milked
cows at dawn and carried sloshing pails
hung from a yoke on shoulders
broadened to the task. She has kneaded fat
mounds of dough, sinking heavy fists deep
into voluptuous bread, innocent
and sensuous as a child in spring mud.
Evenings she mends and patches
the coarse wool of her bodice, smelling
her own sweat, sweet like grass and dung
in the barn or like warm milk
fresh from the udder.

Her world is grained and gritty, deep-
textured, rough-hewn, earth-toned, solid,
simple and crude. Reed and brass and clay,
wheat and flax and plaster turned to human use
have not come far from the loamy fields
where they were mined and gathered. The things
she handles are round and square, tough-
fibered and strong, familiar as flesh to the touch.

The jug rests in her hand like a baby's
bottom. She bends to her task like a mother
tending her child, hand and eye trained
to this work, heart left to its pondering.

How like tenderness, this look
of complete attention, how like a prayer
that blesses these loaves, this milk
(round like this belly, full like this breast),
given daily into her keeping, this handmaid

on whom the light falls,
haloed in white, hallowed by the gaze
that sees her thus, heavy, thick-lipped,
weathered and earthbound, blessed
and full of grace.

Girl

with a

Pearl

Earring

See how she turns to greet what comes,
surprised but untroubled, not quite
welcoming. She looks askance
at one who has, unasking, disturbed her
solitude. Her greeting concedes what it must,
but she remains turned to purposes of her own.

This, too, she will turn to her purposes,
an encounter she expected, not knowing
just when, or what she should expect.
She has kept her own counsel;
it will serve her now.

Breeding has taught her that all-bearing look.
Poised to take what comes, she receives
with grace, gives back what befits
her modesty and station.

Cordelia would have done no more.

Richly presentable in linen and pearls,
wrapped in a light that fits her like her scarves,
she rises to the occasion, self-possessed,
accustomed to possession,
relinquishing solitude with dignity,
who will not be forced,
neither eager nor reluctant,
not defensive, not submissive,
willing to speak her *"Fiat mihi"*
in her own time.

Self-contained, containing months
of loneliness, only the child he left
her with to add its heartbeat to her own,
she wonders, nights when it is cold,
how cold it is in the merchant ship
between ports, on the wintery sea.

Mornings she follows his course
on the wrinkled map that taunts her
with its mute abstractions.

Woman in Blue

A letter has come. She walks
from door to window, holding it
in the light as a jeweler holds
a diamond to the sun. She stands,
though a chair offers its welcome
to limbs and back straining to bear
their burden in these final days of waiting.

It is a feast for hungry
eyes, though only a scant
sea-ration, scribbled in a tavern
in a Spanish port, sent so long ago,
he's already drinking in another.

The child may come before he does,
and the crest of this longing break
and ebb, whose force is gathered
in these clutching hands.

She mouths the words—
few, inelegant, but precious
as the pearls he'll bring
as barter for her patience—
as if whispers could summon
the sound of his seaman's speech
shaping awkward words of love
that lie, rough-cut,
on this silent page, embarrassed
in the light of this frank gaze,
hardly adequate to appease
this appetite, or bear the weight
of all this love.

Woman Writing a Letter

Mid-sentence she looks up, caught
on a snag of thought. Some image
that stills the flow of words holds her
suspended, takes her from this dawn-lit
room, frees her of the weight and pull
of ermine, wool, ribbons, jewels,
into a place where only mind can go,
leaving in token only a
half-smile and wide, still eyes.
The blush on her cheek rises
not in response to the unnoticed gaze
of a witnessing eye, but to an impulse
so inward it seems a trespass
to look too long. Such privacy
forefends disturbance
even as it fascinates the one who,
watching, finds himself
suddenly alone.

Or else she is not caught
by a thought at all, but by the bark
of her small dog who sees a mouse
in the woodpile, or the rustling skirts
of the servant girl who passes
the door with a basket of apples.

Summoned back from a world
she makes of words and memories
by the thumps and clangs of life
to where she is mistress and in the midst
of things, dressed and ready to finish
the letter, let the dog out, instruct
the cook, prepare the guest list, she lifts
her eyes to greet one who calls her,
consents again to this solid world
of things and duties, hesitates only
this one moment to let go some last
reluctance before she rises, puts down
her pen, greets her waiting bridegroom
and shoulders the blessed burden
of these encumbering comforts.

*Young
Woman
with a
Water
Pitcher*

Spring has come and early sunlight
pools on polished surfaces, splays
into color on silver and glass, touches
her fingers and face and arms,
an unction of reawakening.

Perhaps a box of geraniums hangs from the sill
and, preparing their morning draught, she finds
that one has blossomed in the night.

The passing clouds bring no rain now, only
bear the light along, casting benevolent shadows
on lanes and fields, drawing the eye upward again
that has been bent all winter to the book or the fire
as the huddled body conserved its warmth
and early darkness drove the spirit inward.

Look how her body opens now:
arms that were folded spread wide, face
turned to the light like the sturdy petals
of her northern flowers that peek from thick stems
and heavy leaves, reasserting color
after months of drab—pinks and yellows
and mottled greens that bless the eye as light
submits in them to the terms of form and substance.

And this solid girl, radiant flesh emerging
from skirts and stays, veil and cuffs and collar,
reaches for air and water, forsaking her worldly tasks
to choose the better part—to pray
the prayer of the grateful body, drink in
the light that illumines her, and reclaim the moment
from its dailiness, hushed like an acolyte who bears
the sacred gifts and awaits the transformation.

They say a man's figure once filled the doorway,
but the painter repented and now only light
from a far room draws the eye beyond red
rugs and ripe fruit and flushed girl, sleeping.

But the open door disturbs the eye and turns
the mind to speculation: Who has seen her here?
Who might? What does she neglect? Or wait for
wearily? And why does it feel discourteous
to witness such unself-conscious sleep?

A Girl
Asleep

Scents of peaches and poured wine have worked
their magic. Silent, the afternoon has drawn
its shadows over her with unseen hands,
shaping the landscape of her dream
while day descends to darkness.

Soon enough she'll waken to the call
of a voice or chill of a passing breeze
or a step on the vacant threshold
will break the spell that holds her here
in such precarious peace.

The course is called "Portraiture
in Literature and Art." The students stare
at Vermeer's young woman on the wall.

The teacher turns from the portrait
to the circle of faces before her.
"What does the painter see?" she asks.
"What does he want us to see?"
"What do we know about her? About him?"

Portrait of a Young Woman

A young man speaks: "She's young and chaste.
And nothing bad has happened to her yet."

An older woman shakes her head. She knows
this look; she's mothered them and taught them
all for fifteen years—young girls who want
to please—on some points, anyway.
Now in school herself again,
free at last to look and linger
over fine distinctions, free to say
what life has taught, she speaks in turn:

"Look at that smile. Think how early
she has learned to pose and please
and give, but not too much.
She's patient. She will have to be. But see
what intellect is there—the eyebrows raised,
the mouth upturned—and what restraint.
Think of all that is withheld, what won't be shared.
Child that she is, she has her secrets. Docile
to her elders, still she'll never tell
that man, or us, what occupies her thoughts
while she sits and gazes at the easel's back."

A younger woman disagrees.
"I think this is his daughter," she suggests,
softly so that half the class must ask her
"What?" and so she tries again: "I think she is
the painter's child, pleased to be picked
from among the crowd. Didn't you say
Vermeer had eleven children?"

("Almost a third as many," the teacher thinks,
as the paintings he produced. "And if
they were all like this, then who can say
which was the greater work?")

"Think if you were only one among so many,"
she goes on. "Think if your father gazed at you
alone for an hour or more, and saw you with such
scrutiny, your very soul would rise to meet him,
how you'd swear obedience, stifle every
rebel thought, and only hope
that someday some man might take time
to see you with such utter care again."

An older man, for whom these evening classes
offer respite from legal briefs and clients'
complaints, always waits as if to see
that all returns are in before
he ventures judgment. Then he interjects,
head cocked, half-smiling,
"And what about the painter? Haven't we
been asked to think what we can know of him?"

Before he speaks a further word, a woman says,
"He loves her," and another, "No, she's only
an ideal. Another in the endless line of Blessed
Virgins, not a one who looks the way a woman
sees herself." Another speaks: "There's nothing
here but her—where's the room, the window,
wine glass, lute, or letter? Not a prop, no light
source—I would call this worship. No one exists the way
this woman does, in time alone. Where is the space
she occupies? And how do we know
what moment she's been caught in? Artifice
like this is adoration, and the artist is in awe."

The teacher watches all the faces looking
at the girl. "Think again," she says,
"how art can show us to ourselves.
We see the way we are. We need,
each one of us, more than two eyes to see
what the human face can tell, or read
what the hand inscribes." She takes the picture
off the wall and glances at the clock.

"Go home. Write about her now.
 Give her lines and let her speak. Put her
on the stage or in the street. And never
see a woman's face again without
at least a passing thought of what
one man with eyes to see her
found in hers."

Woman with a Lute

Not only preparation
for performance or lesson:
tuning the lute is a pleasure
all its own.

See how she leans to listen,
ear to her instrument, eyes
to the light as if, looking hard,
she might see the sound
approaching its perfect pitch
like a bird about to alight
on a sapling's smallest branch.

Fine tuning instrument and ear,
this keen listening is her learning.
Here, in her hour away from the world,
she schools herself in subtlety,
practices precision, patiently
restoring order and measure,
finding what string and wood require,
weaving wave and particle, until
the two are one.

Lady
Writing
a Letter
with Her
Maid

In my dream I am both women:
the one who writes and the one who waits.

Urgently, as if the sun will set
before she has brought her words to bear
upon some business long delayed,
the writer leans to her lines,
flushed and focused,
as if her work depends upon
the lingering of this fading light—
as if, indeed, neglecting this,
nothing else would fully matter.

Blissfully beyond the day's distractions
in single-minded solitude rich
with the rush of feeling that urges her fingers
across the page, she is for this bright moment
pure of heart, willing one thing.

The one who waits doesn't want
to write. She watches
the passing shapes of summer clouds,
a neighbor hanging sheets to dry,
a child kicking rattling stones
along a cobbled street. She is
as true to her repose as the writer
to her task. This is her work: to wait.

The writer, who has forgotten her,
can only work when she is there.
The waiting woman keeps her post,
stands between her mistress and the muse,
holding the center, looking toward the source
of light, contained and content to keep
her wordless vigil.

*Officer
and
Laughing
Girl*

One more dark soldier, like the Moor,
tells a woman tales and takes
in the mirror of her face the measure
of his wit. Loving him, he thinks,
"for the dangers he has passed," he loves her
"that she pities them."

Thus windows become mirrors and the glittering
image of one's own face obscures the mystery
and the gift that lies beyond the looking glass.

Giving him what he wants, she reserves the rest
for someone who wants more.

He thinks she's charmed. She is amused.
He thinks she wishes "heaven had made her
such a man" that she might travel the world
whose curves and hollows stretch like Urbino's lady
on the wall. But here, in her shaft of sunlight, she has
world enough, and time.

She harbors desires beyond his guessing,
contentment deeper than desire.

Light cradles her like a lover's hand. It is enough.
His delight in her delight in him takes no account
of her deep pleasure drawn from a source
he cannot know, who has only the wide world
for his dwelling place.

Girl
Reading
a Letter
at an
Open
Window

Afternoon light falls
on ochres and reds and pale golds.
Velvets and linens and wools
sway heavily in the light
breeze that passes through
this bower of abundance.

The letter she holds has been read before.
Pulling taut the wrinkled sheet she reads
again what she could now recite.
The words on which her gaze falls so intently
reach from the page like a familiar touch,
tender and faint as the delicate script
bleached by the light of this autumn afternoon.

Perhaps it is from an absent husband, running
the trade that brought these rugs a thousand miles,
and bought this fruit, best of the harvest, for her table.

Perhaps not. It may be she who has gone away.
Given in marriage beyond what she knew to hope for,
taken from the sound of known feet on the village path,
from a circle of friends gathered to gossip
at the brookside after the day's tasks,
from the mother who writes her now, wondering
whether, in her grand house, among her servants
and soft garments, she still cares for news from home.

Not even her mother knows how much
she cares: how she is glad that the old, blind cobbler's
young apprentice is kind to him, and repairs
without a word the vagrant stitches on sole and tongue,
and calls him father; that her sister is learning
to weave and has taken her place reading verses
after the evening meal; that the little hunchback still rides
on the peddler's cart and laughs back
at the children who laugh at him.

The streets of this city are silent as her ear strains
for familiar sounds. No woman's voice summons her
in this household where, as yet, there is no babe
to cry or nurse to scold. The man who adores her
knows her only as his lady.

None of them knows how she would like, some evenings,
to lay her coiffed head on a breast broader and softer than her own;
to bake, mornings, in a kitchen crowded with bowls and chatter;
to strip off her fine-stitched shoes and wade in a muddy brook
in secret, skirts gathered, with a giggling friend
in the heat and falling light of the afternoon.

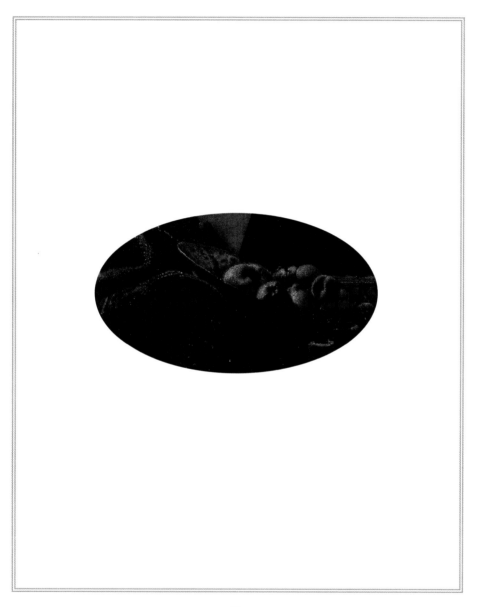

Mistress and Maid

Subtler than they seem—
the ties that bind
mistress to maid—more
than money: secrets
entrusted and kept, delicate
decorums of the boudoir
observed, closeted
camaraderie sustained.

Maid looks upon mistress
with amusement so veiled,
it might pass for benevolence—
or the pity of one who knows
the pleasures of the lower born
and knows the high and hidden cost
of pearls, ermine, and concealment.

The mistress gazes at the maid
or past her into darkness,
perplexed, or undecided, or
distracted by a second thought.
She knows how households thrive
on well-managed passions. She keeps
her counsel and her confidante
keeps her peace.

Few words pass between them,
but those that fill the pages fly
from this table like falcons sent to trace
their circles on the morning breeze.

Passion, like the shock of red
beneath her gaping cloak,
runs its narrow course
in a life of domestic duty.
Feeling finds its way.
Friendships thrive on fancy.
And though this genteel burgher's wife
tends, Bianca-like, the wishes of her lord,
her pen and private thoughts remain her own.

Allegory of Painting

He has learned to mix his powders, draw
his brush to a hair's breadth, translate
light to shades of white and gold, and
fill the shadows with suggestion.

She, too, has learned her trade: still
standing where an hour ago he placed her,
book and instrument angled to satisfy
his cool, exacting eye, she bears,
with the weight of props and crown
and copious garb, the burden of being,
for him, and for the passing connoisseur,
myth, muse, ideal, idea, mirage—
not, in any case, herself.

Acting her part in this quiet theater
for an audience of one, and he preoccupied
with matters of perspective and proportion,
she claims her art as he does his.

Being herself, the part she plays
will never be quite what he imagined.
The life she brings to this stiff role
incarnates an idea; her vision
revises his. The story the canvas tells
will have her heartbeat in it, her face,
her self a source of light,
unextinguished by heavy costume,
and hard scrutiny. In these long hours
that make the body ache she learns
how to claim her power
in compliance.

The Girl with the Red Hat

It's been an hour already;
the collar itches, the silk
keeps sliding. My neck is tired
and I've heard enough
apprentices' chatter about
this hat.

Outside I hear the rattle
of the farmer's cart. I'll miss
the boy who brings butter
and cheeses—so many
to choose from.

I'll have no say in the matter—
Boerenkaas, Edam, Gouda—
the others are nibbling even now,
while I sit here in
this hat.

You're devoted to your trade,
the tools you keep so clean, the boys
who pay to paint with you. For me,
it's only duty. I'd rather be washing
linens in the sun, strolling
by the canal, my hair loose in the wind,

than watching you watch me
sit still while you sketch
and talk textures and peer
over the easel, considering
shades of red for lips and cheeks
and, above all, the real feast
for the viewer's eye—
this hat.

You don't ask me what I think,
but I amuse myself imagining
how when we're done I'll drop it
into the Oude Langendijk and watch
it float away, startling the ducks,
getting some entertainment,
after all, from
this red hat.

Woman with a Pearl Necklace

It seems a permissible pleasure,
forgivable vanity in one so young,
to love the beauty of her pearls
and petal skin, to set apart
a moment in midday to revel
in luxury and loveliness
and find them good.

See how she holds her necklace to the light.
Later it will lie on her bosom,
ignored with the studied disregard
of maiden modesty, adding one more curve
to the calculus of breast and cheek and chin
and wayward curl, others looking,
she the looked upon.

But in this hour alone, before the sun
retreats to night, the room to shadow, and she
to those who await her courtesies, she may indulge
the heavenly, earthly impulse
to gaze and take delight.

Given another time and place this face
might serve some artist for a nun's,
rapt in attention, stilled before an image
not unlike her own.

Woman Holding a Balance

Between light and dark,
between this world and the next,
between maidenhood and motherhood
she pauses, held in balance
like the balance she holds.

Her focus not the gold or
the weighing, but the justice
of her scales, settling to their still
point in a steady hand,
and she herself unadorned,
a lily that needs no gilding
but the points of light that lie
on her veil like jewels on a crown.

If she raised her eyes, she would see
this luminous beauty, drop the scales,
and, like a blushing Eve, break
the balance and forsake
the innocence of her task,
but she does not.

If she turned, she would see
the Last Judgment, saints and sinners
weighed in the final balance, and,
called to think on ultimate things,
lose this moment—
but she does not.

Trained on the object, undistracted,
patient while the instrument swings
to its center and is still, she turns
this little task to prayer—if mindfulness is
prayer—to an exercise of love—if it is love
to be attentive to the thing at hand.

*Life
Drawing:
Advanced
Beginners*

The teacher stands at her easel, naked man
behind her, half turned from the light.

"You have learned about line and form," she begins,
"how faces have shapes—the oval, the heart,
the sharp-jawed square—how we work
from ideal proportions—an eye's breadth
between the eyes, Leonardian ratios measuring
joint to joint.

"Now you must learn where the shadow goes.

"There is no soul without shadow—only surface
and suggestion. But see, when we darken
the hollowed cheek, shade beneath these eyes
that have read too long or seen too much, we begin
to think of the life of a man."

Her pencil traces the body and we learn
what lines and shadows have to teach: imitation
is fidelity to more than form. Revelation lies
in what the consenting eye may see, and praise
in the hand that is faithful to that seeing.

She speaks as she moves along the limbs:
"See how we know what these arms can do:
the weight they have borne is defined by this darkness.

"Ask yourself," she tells us, "Where is the light
that illumines this body? What is hidden?
Half-hidden? What lies open to our gaze?
What is left to guessing?

"Consider technique: some do the shadow in shades of gray,
graphite or charcoal spread with the fingers the way
we move our hands over a face we love, finding
its curves like the blind learning to see, seeking
what will not come to words.
                              Some score the surface
with tiny lines. Close up they look like scars.

"Every body," she reminds us, "is a story. Tell it.
The story is in the shadow."

LIST OF ILLUSTRATIONS

Page 42: *Woman with a Lute*, c. 1664, The Metropolitan Museum of Art, New York, Bequest of Collis P. Huntington, 1900. Courtesy of The Metropolitan Museum of Art.

Page 44: *Lady Writing a Letter with Her Maid*, c. 1670, National Gallery of Ireland, Dublin. Courtesy of Giraudon/Art Resource, NY.

Page 46: *Officer and Laughing Girl*, c. 1657, The Frick Collection, New York. Courtesy of The Frick Collection.

Page 48: *Girl Reading a Letter at an Open Window*, c. 1657, Staatliche Kunstsammlungen Dresden, Gemäldegalerie Alte Meister. Courtesy of Lessing/Art Resource, NY.

Page 51: Detail of *Girl Reading a Letter at an Open Window*.

Page 52: *Mistress and Maid*, c. 1667, The Frick Collection, New York. Courtesy of The Frick Collection.

Page 55: Detail of *Mistress and Maid*.

Page 56: *Allegory of Painting*, c. 1666-1667, Kunsthistorisches Museum, Vienna. Courtesy of Lessing/Art Resource, NY.

Page 58: *Girl with the Red Hat*, c. 1665-1666, National Gallery of Art, Washington, Andrew W. Mellon Collection. Courtesy of the National Gallery of Art.

Page 61: Detail of *Girl with the Red Hat*.

Page 62: *Woman with a Pearl Necklace*, c. 1664, Staatliche Museen zu Berlin—Preussischer Kulturbesitz Gemäldegalerie.

Page 64: *Woman Holding a Balance*, c. 1664, National Gallery of Art, Washington, Widener Collection. Courtesy of the National Gallery of Art.

Page 66: Detail of *Allegory of Painting*.

Page 68: Detail of *Lady Writing a Letter with Her Maid*.